AF406110

DEDICATIONS

From Jerry

To my loving daughter, Jennifer Ellen Noran (whose name is difficult to turn into an anagram because of its preponderance of N's and E's).

From Jenny

To my amazing Dad, Jerry Noran, who raised me on Dad jokes and the knowledge that I could be whatever I wanted to be, without limitations.

Noran, Jerald E.
A is for Edelweiss: An Absurdist Abecedarium

ISBN: 979-8-9902681-0-4 (hardcover)
ISBN: 979-8-9902681-1-1 (ebook)

1) HUMOR/Form/Limericks & Verse
2) POETRY/Subjects & Themes/General
3) HUMOR/Topic/Art & Literature

First edition published in 2025 by Dragonfly Press Publishing
First printing

For inquiries about volume orders, please contact:
Dragonfly Press Publishing
publisher@dflypress.com
www.dflypress.com

Published in the United States by Dragonfly Press Publishing
Distributed by IngramSpark

Illustrated by Jennifer Noran
www.dflypress.com/jennifernoran

Author photo credit: LIAM
www.instagram.com/blood_tear

10 9 8 7 6 5 4 3 2 1
Printed in the United States of America

A is for Edelweiss: An Absurdist Abecedarium

Written by Jerald E. Noran
Illustrated by Jennifer Noran

A is for edelweiss, blossom of 'sno
('Sno A in edelweiss, didn't you know?).

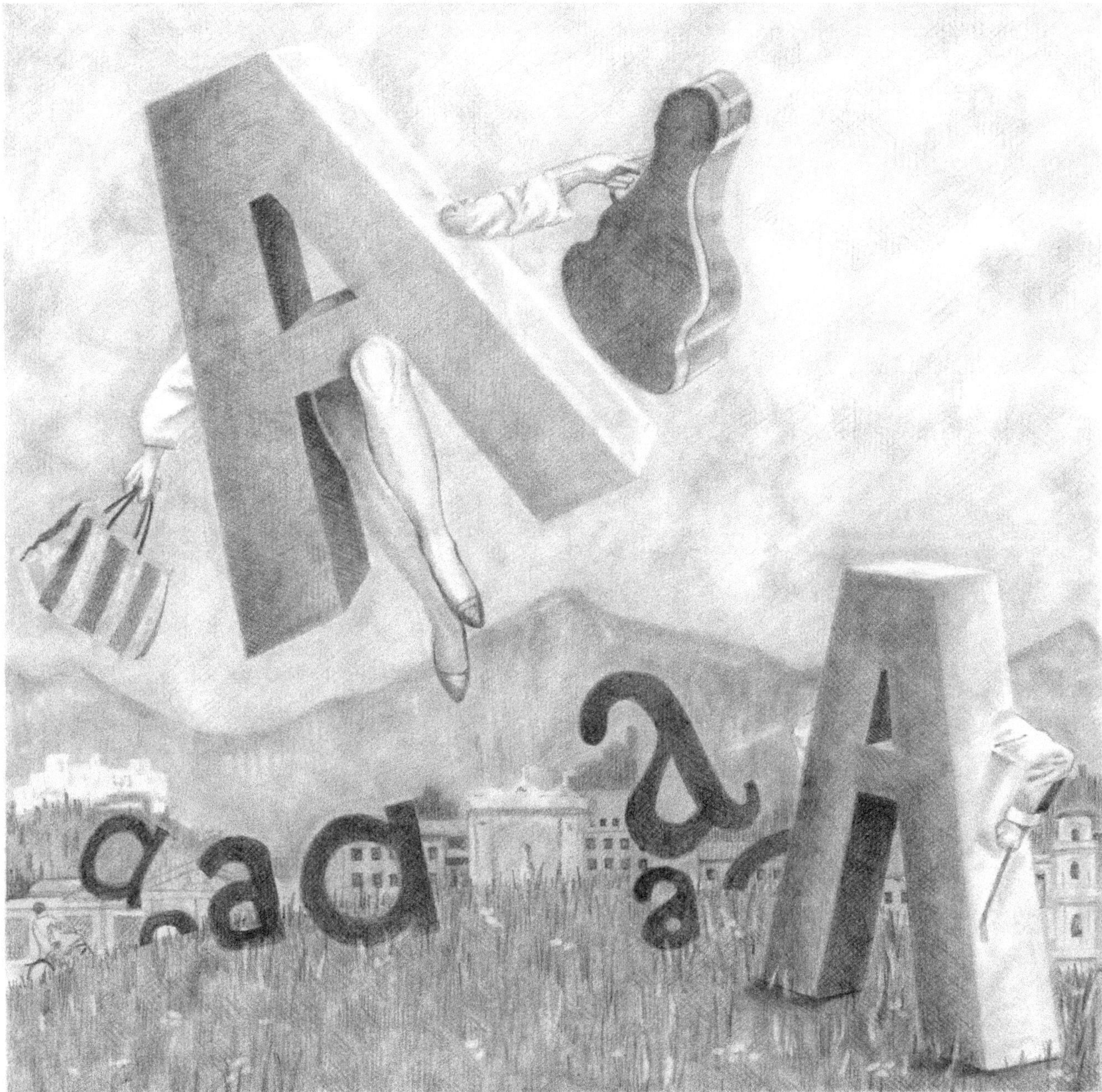

B is in doubt about being in debt;
To be or not…I don't hear two B's yet.

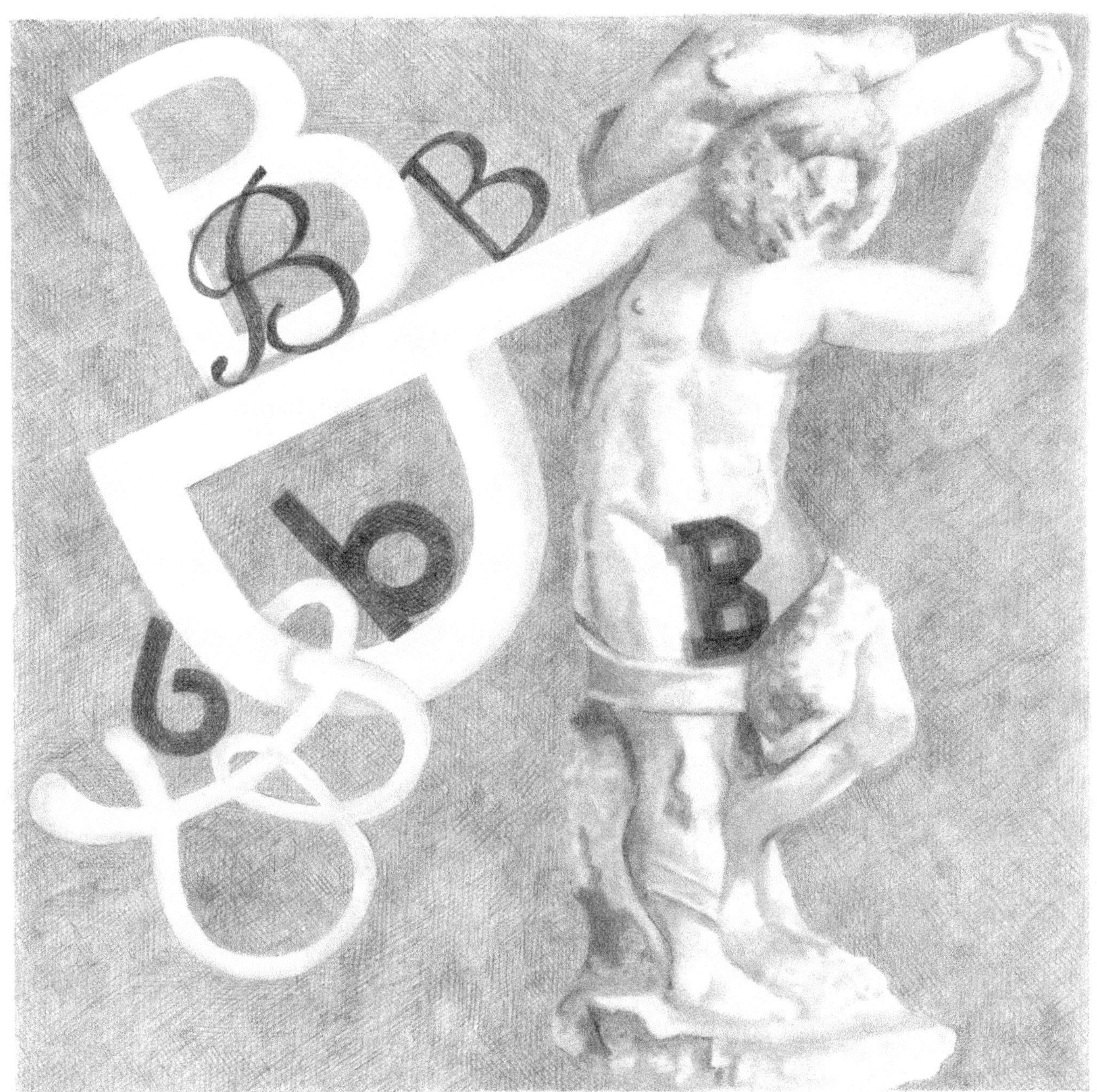

Oh say can you see any sensible reason,
You don't see at least one or two C's in season?

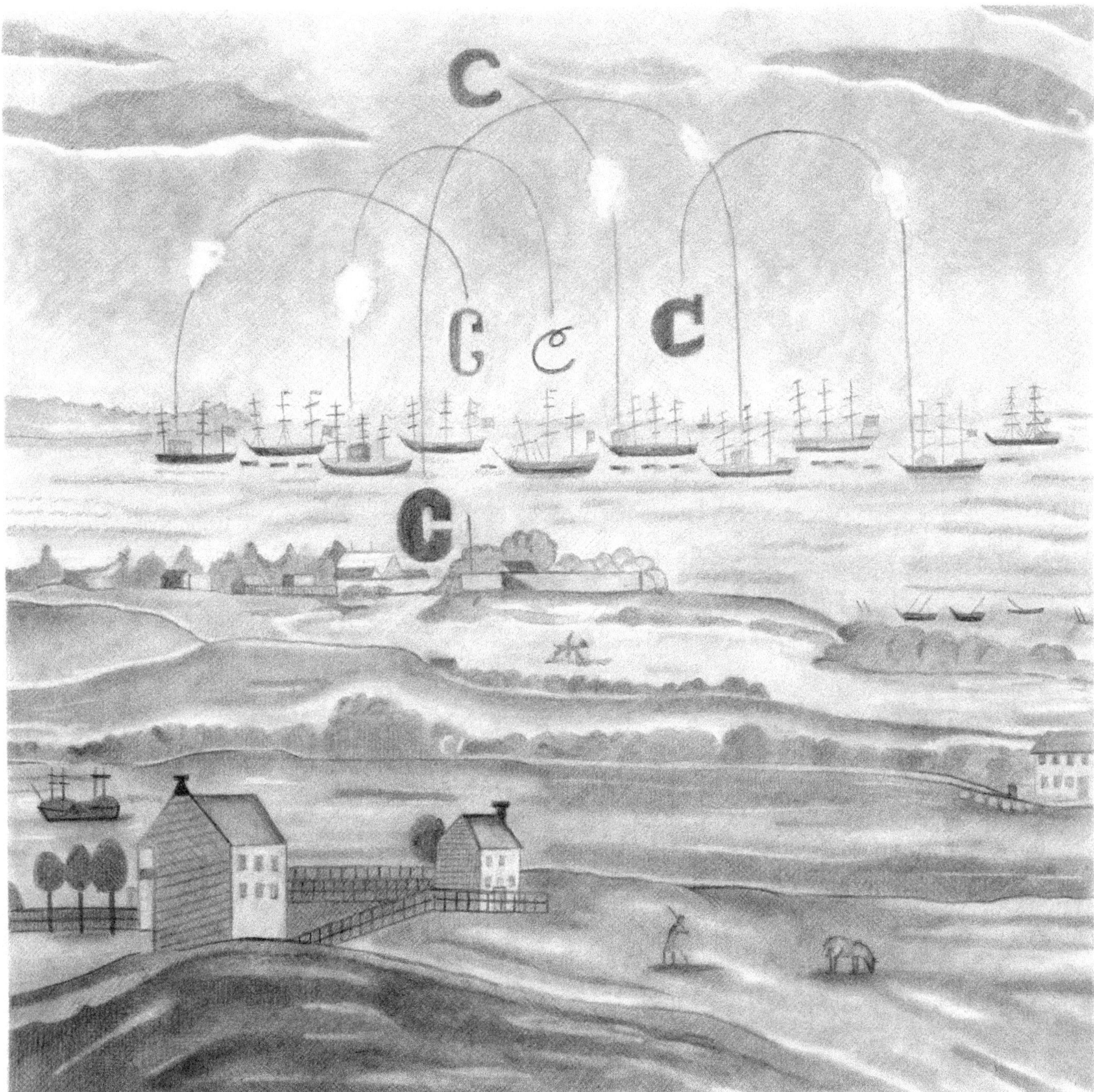

Den, dose guys said de bossman decided dat D's
Should replace all dem H's preceded by T's.

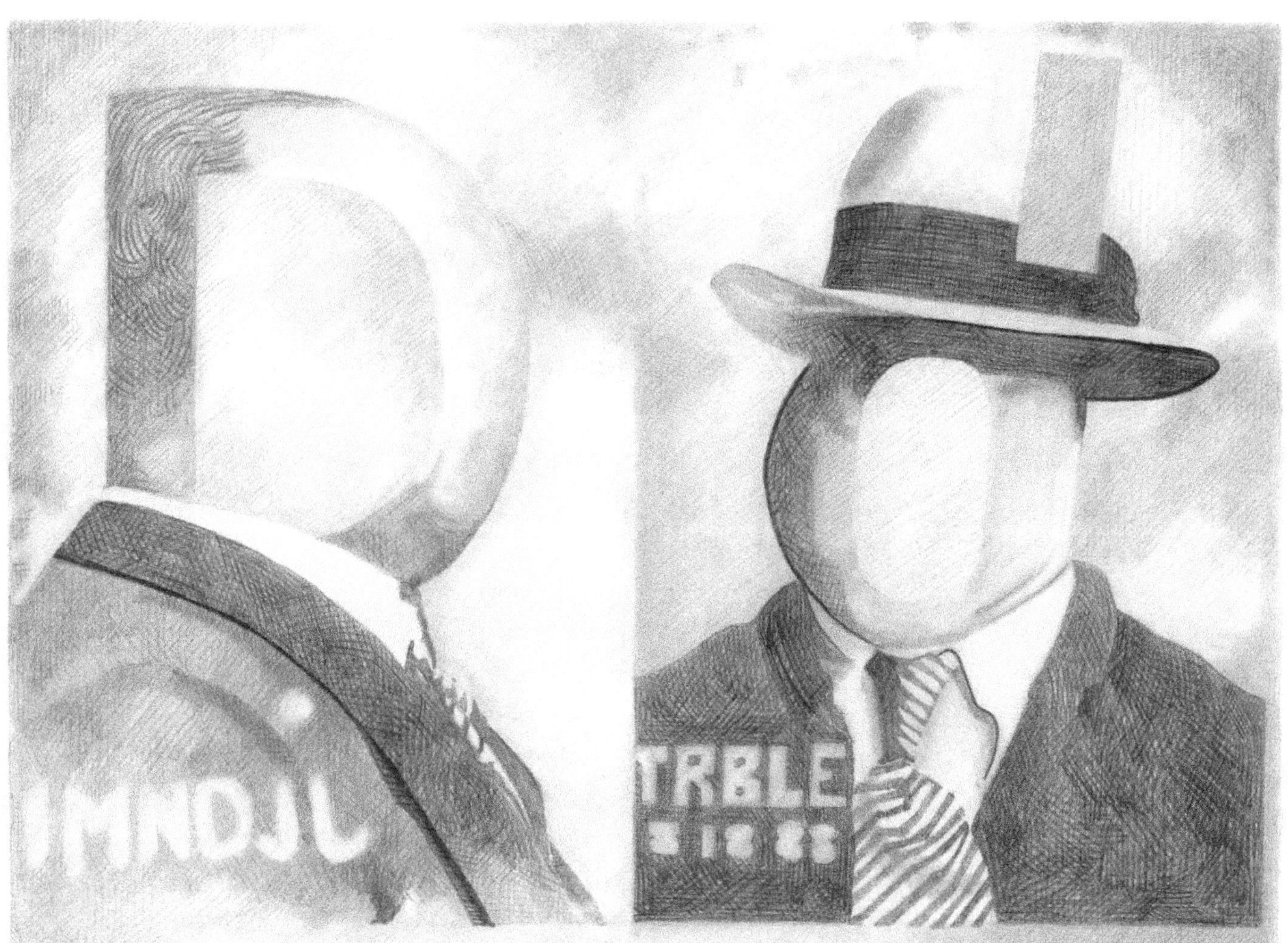

MNDJ
TRBLE
5 19 85

Friends, Romans, Countrymen; E is for ir-
Regardless of anything else you may hear.

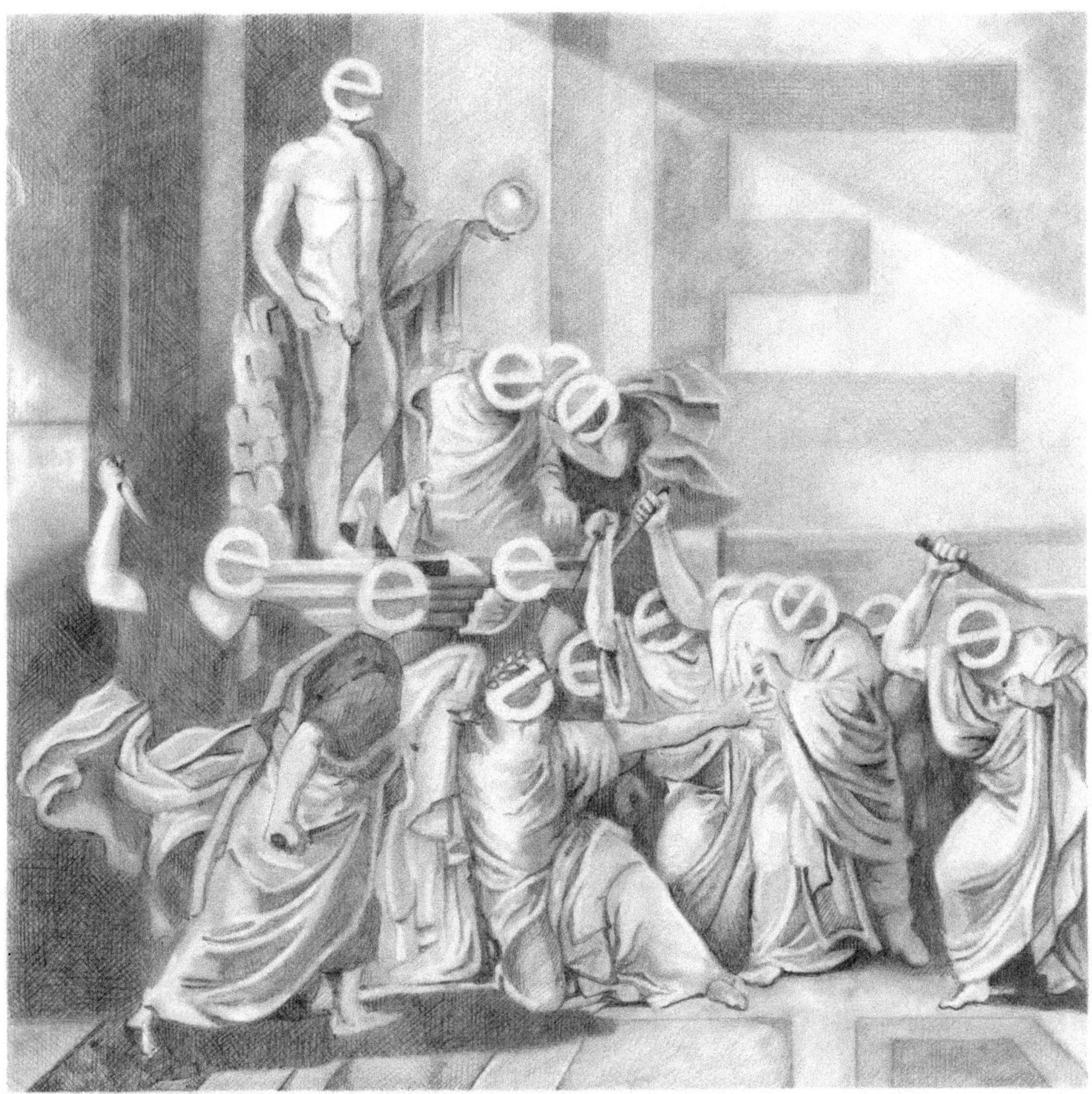

F is ephemeral; it won't live on.
One moment it's here, and the next...

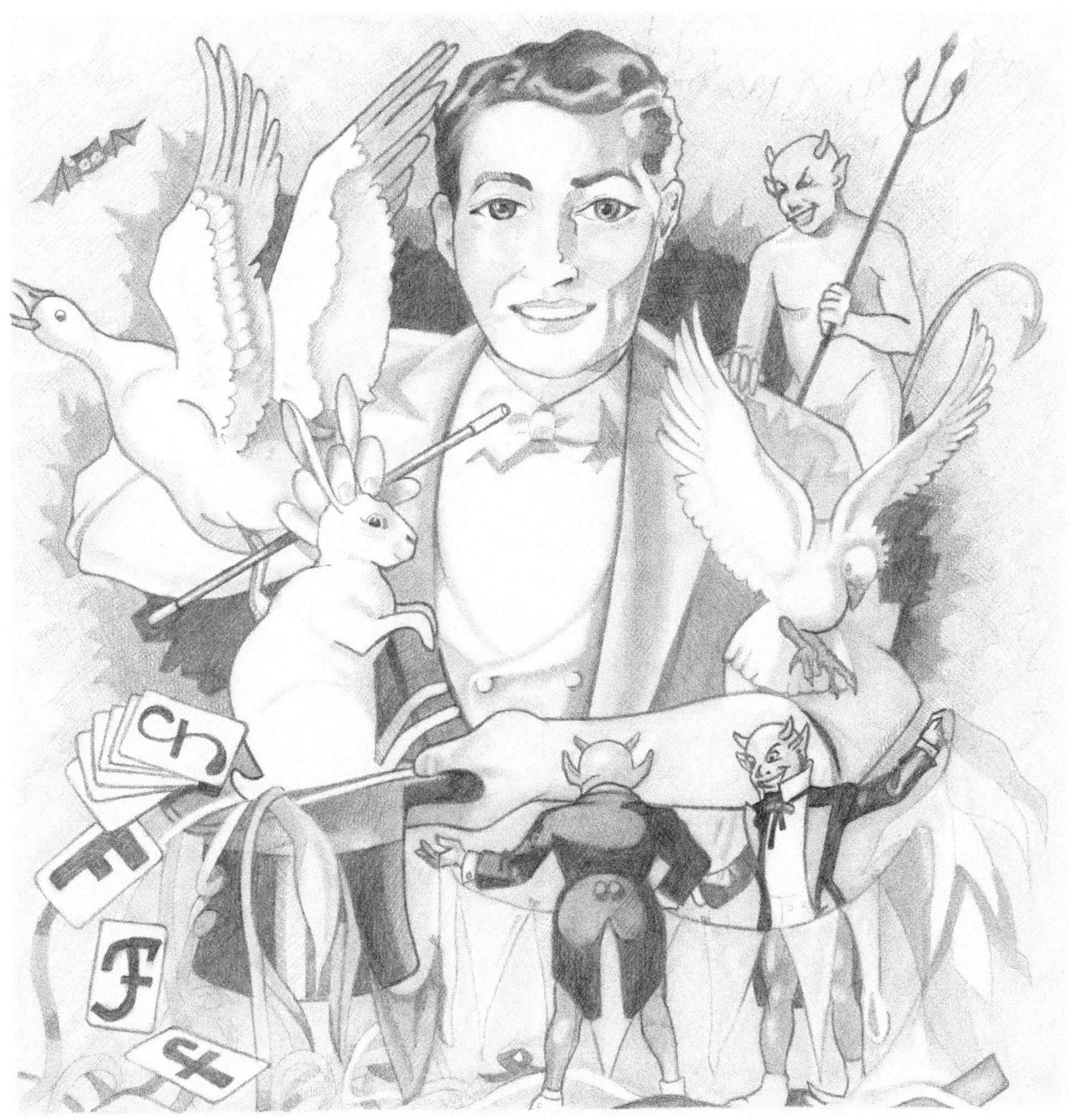

G is for jeans; the kind that are blue.
The Fugates of Hazard wear new blue genes, too.

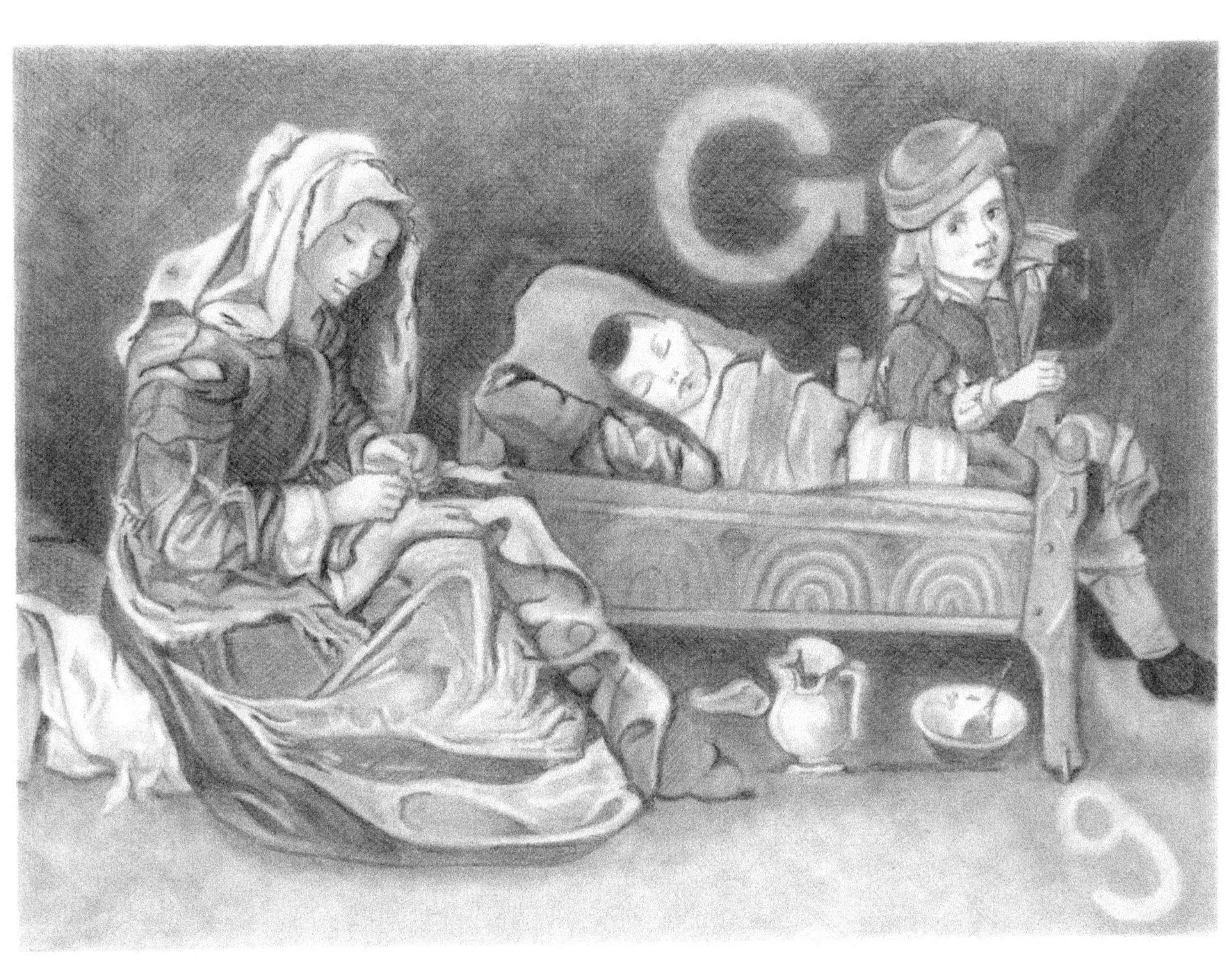

H is for Ajax. This warrior great
Is also well known for inventing Troy wt.

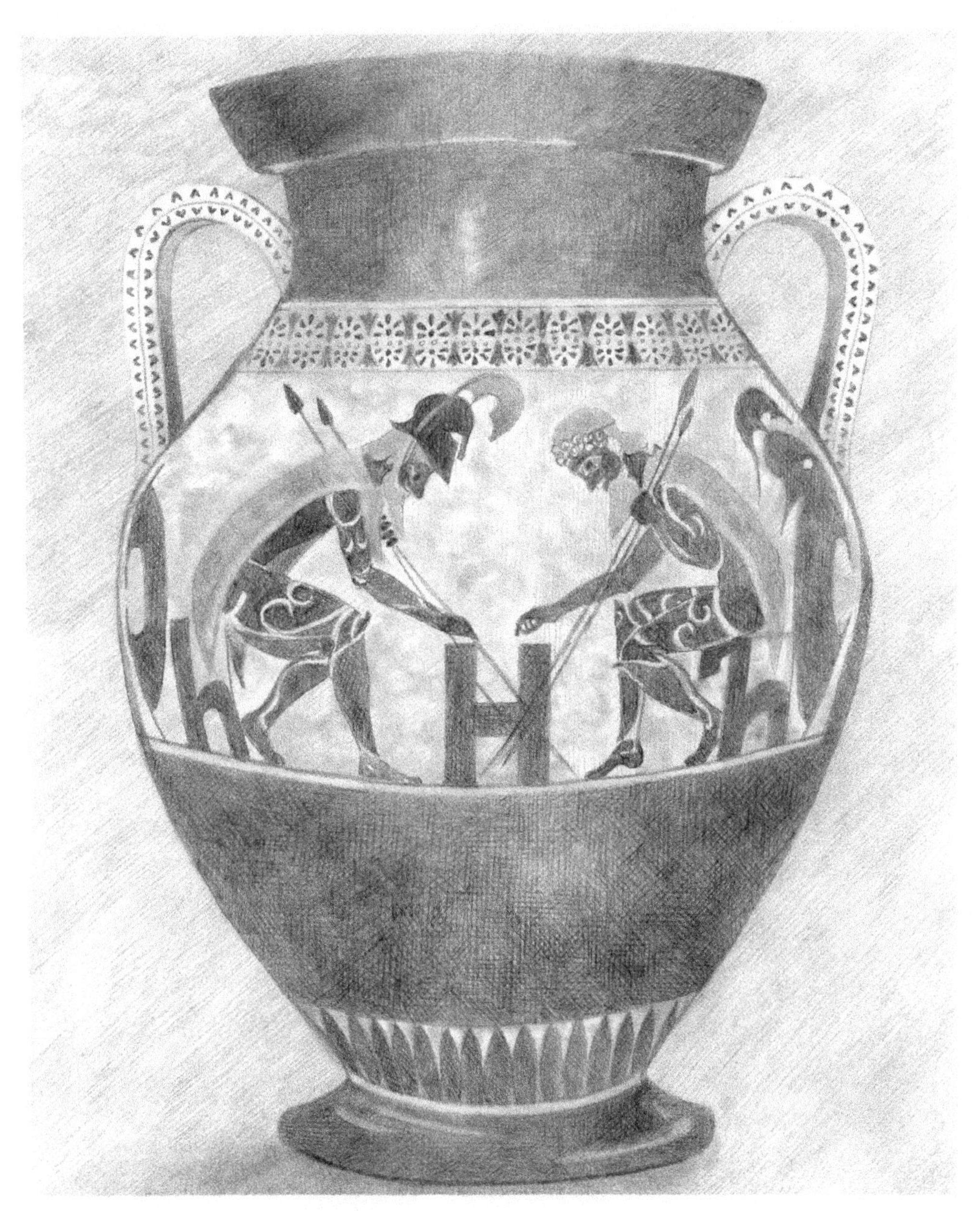

A tooth for a tooth, but no I for an eye.
Aye, to tell you the truth, I don't really know why.

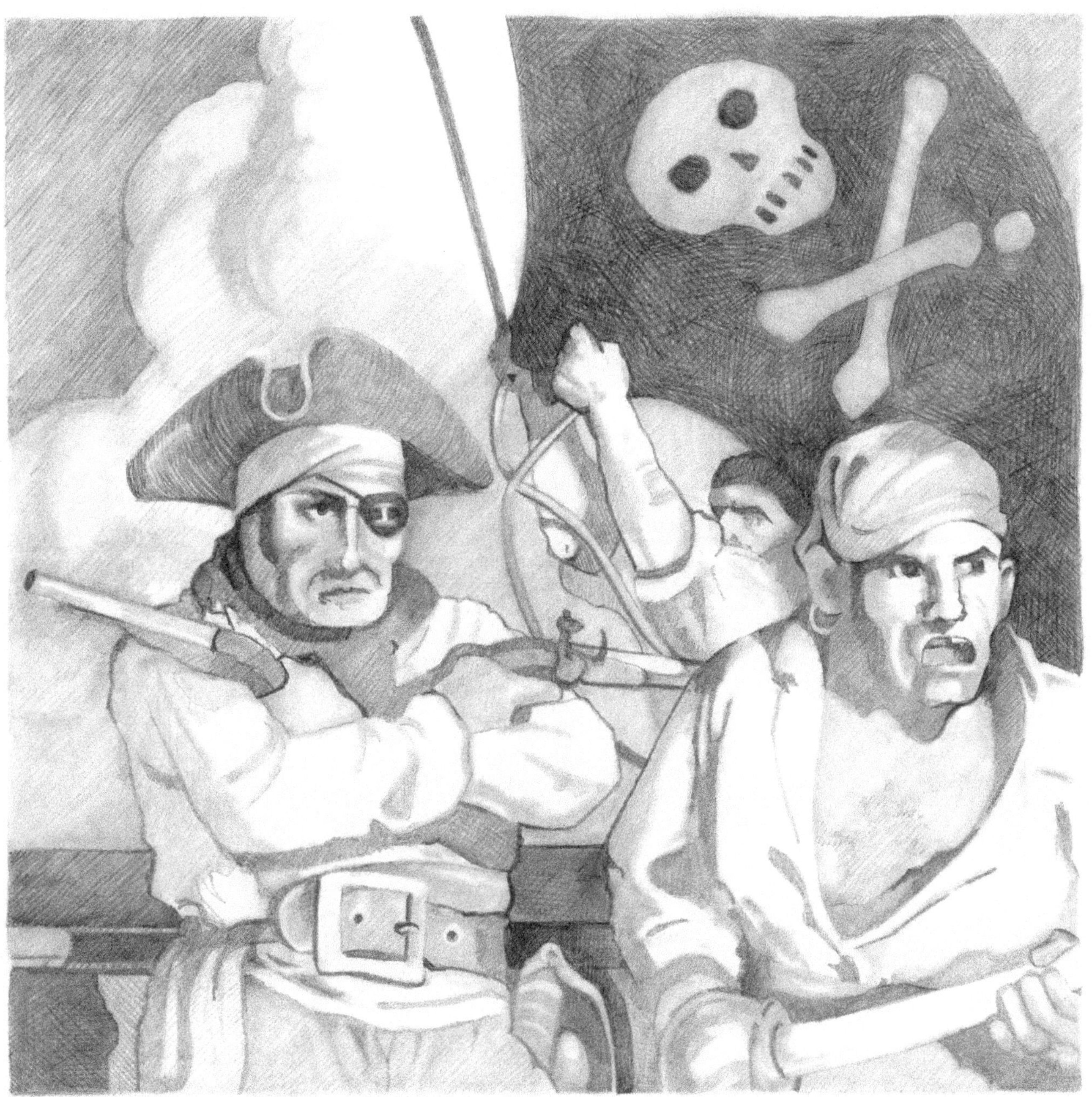

J is for gerund. Is seeing believing?
When nouns look like verbs, then discerning's deceiving.

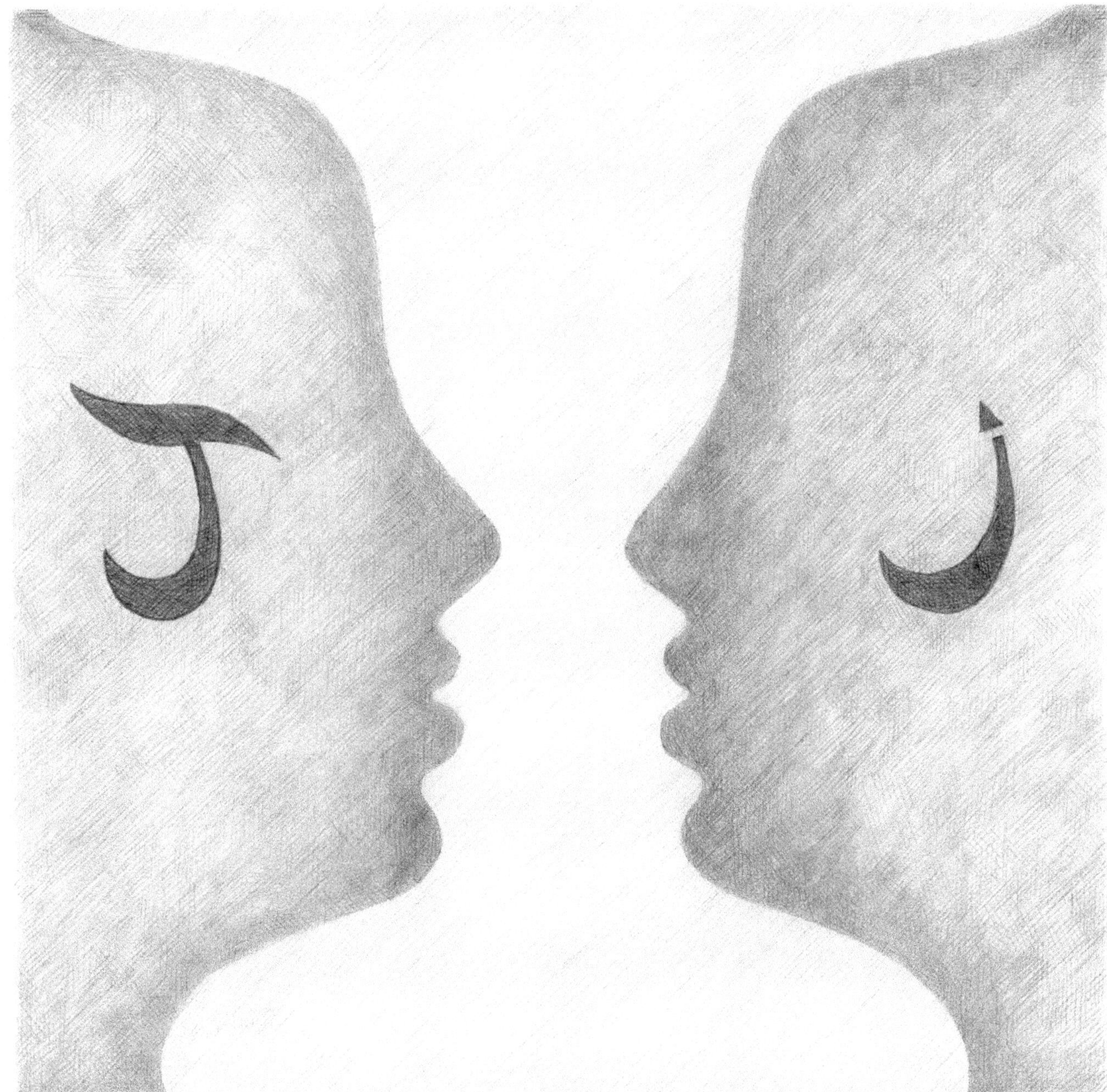

K is for Cain; his brother is Abel.
Cain raises cane, but Abel's not able.
When Cain razes Abel, God raises cain.
Then kith and kin start up all over again.

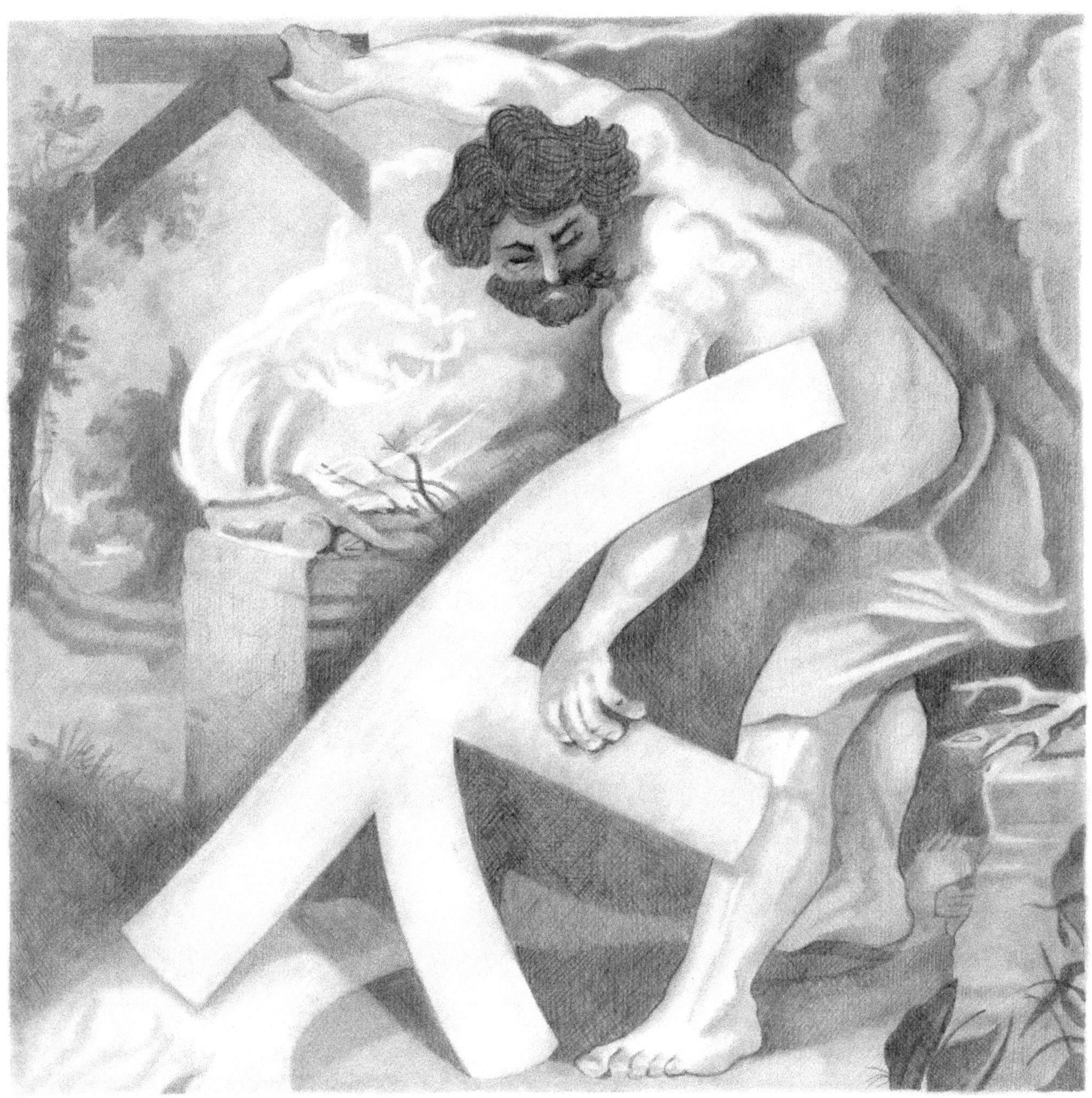

LMN. "Could you now, Holmes, construct for me, please,
A word that begins with three letters like these?"
"Elementary, Watson, I'll do it with E's."

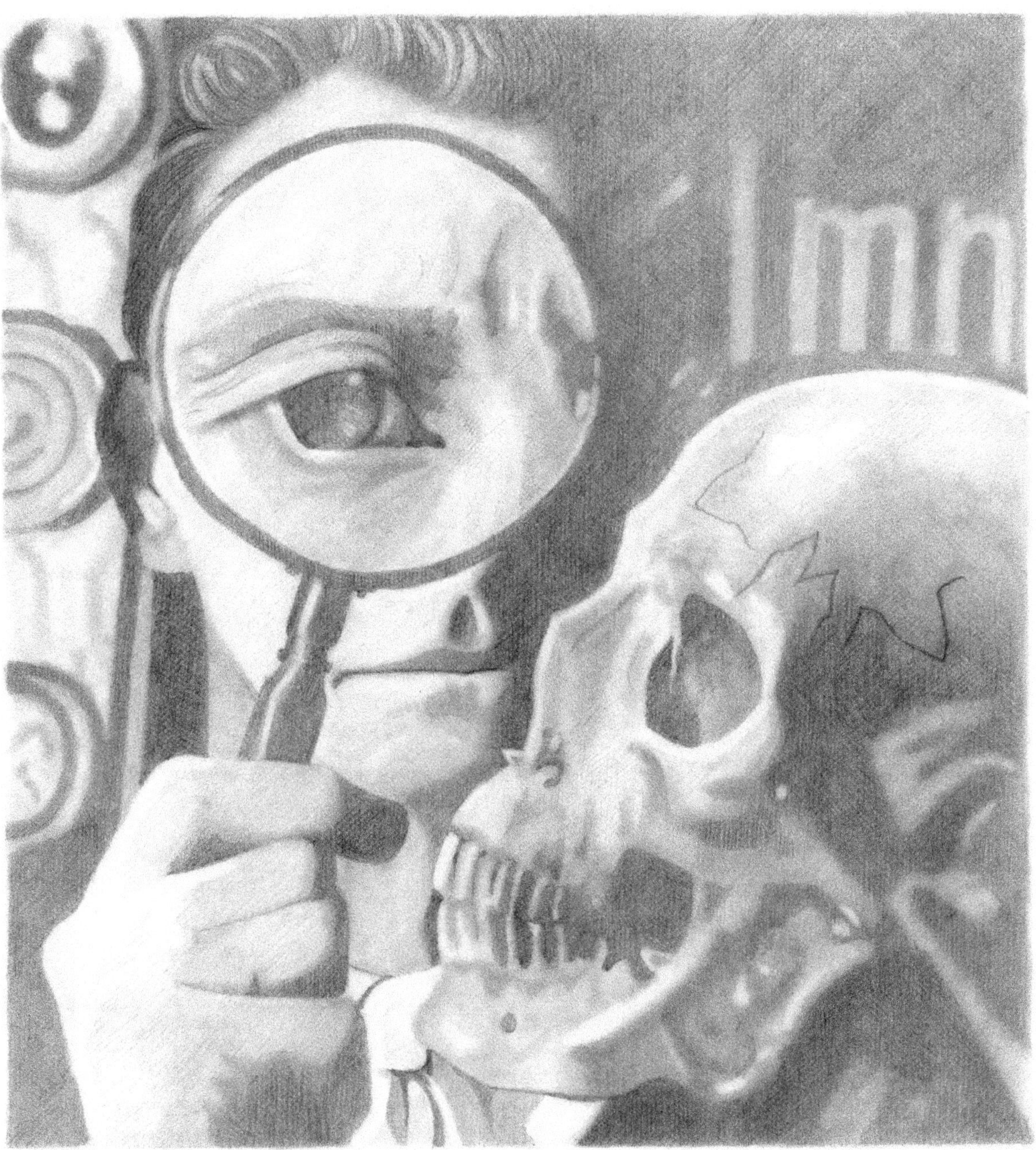
lmn

O? Au revoir. The directions weren't clear.
I thought oral by mouth; they meant aural by ear.

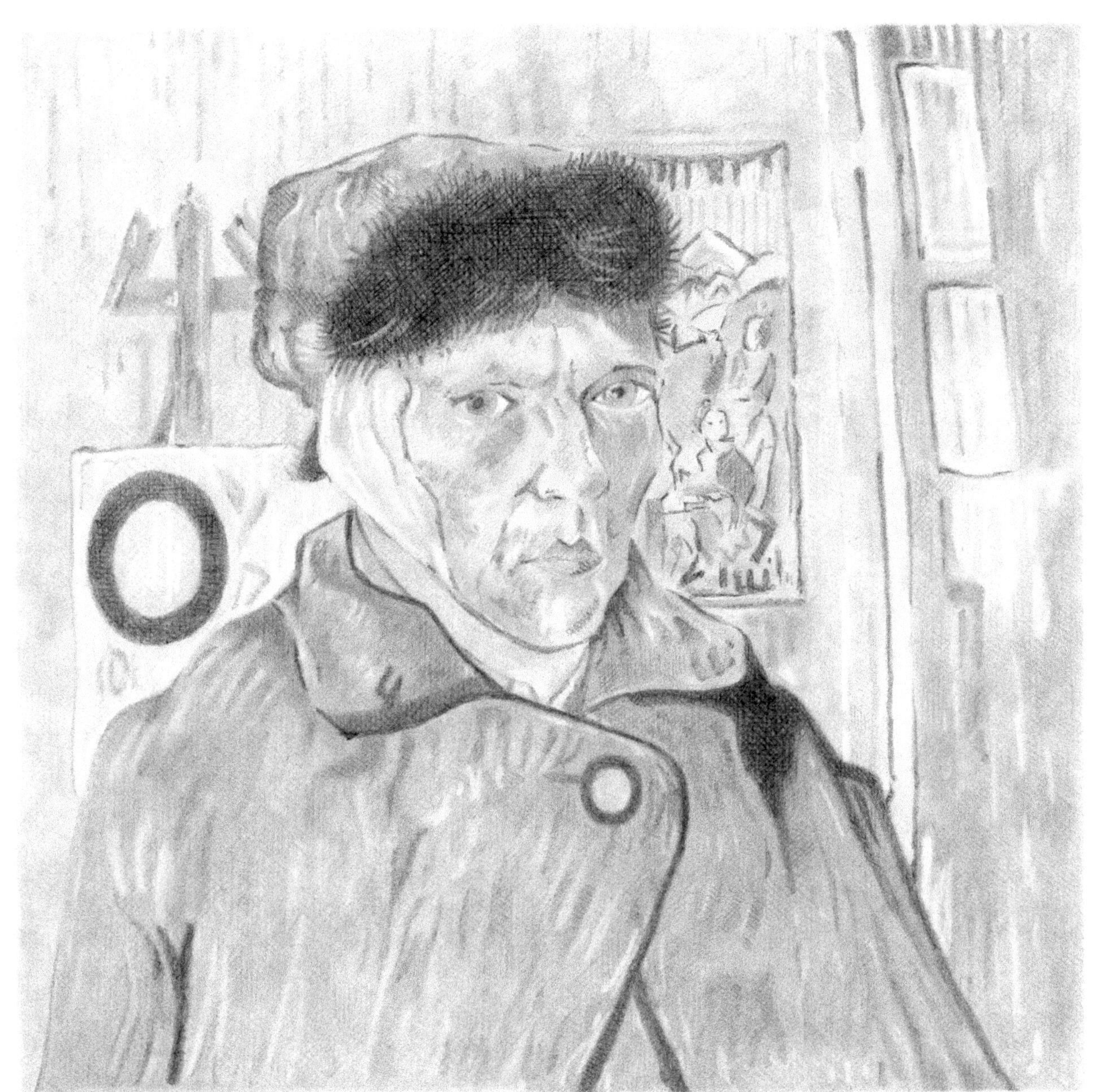

Ptomaine, pneumonia, psoriasis, phlegm.
P is the letter that starts all of them.

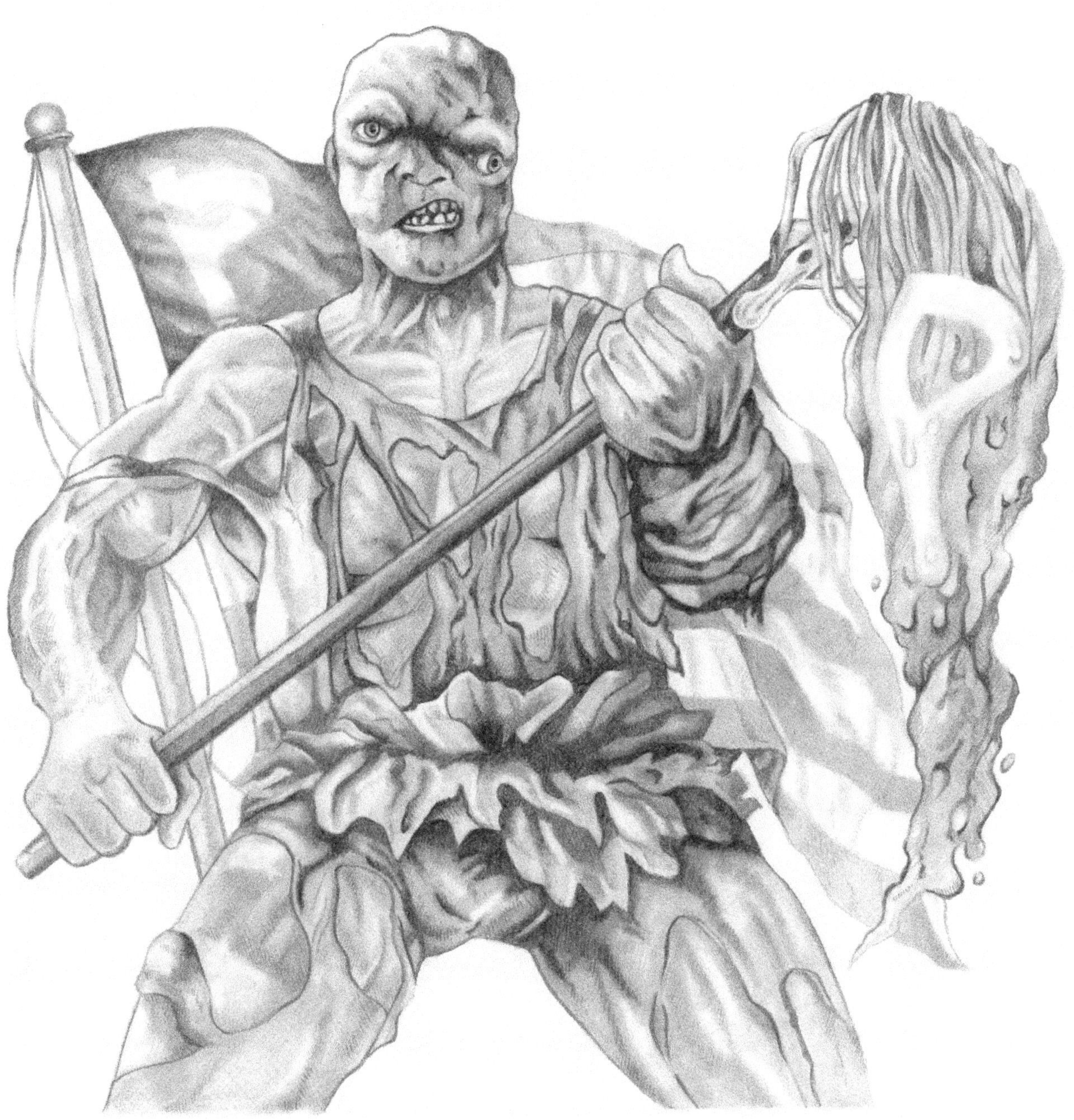

If I is for eyeballs, then Q is for cueballs
(When I write "I is", does it seem my IQ falls?).

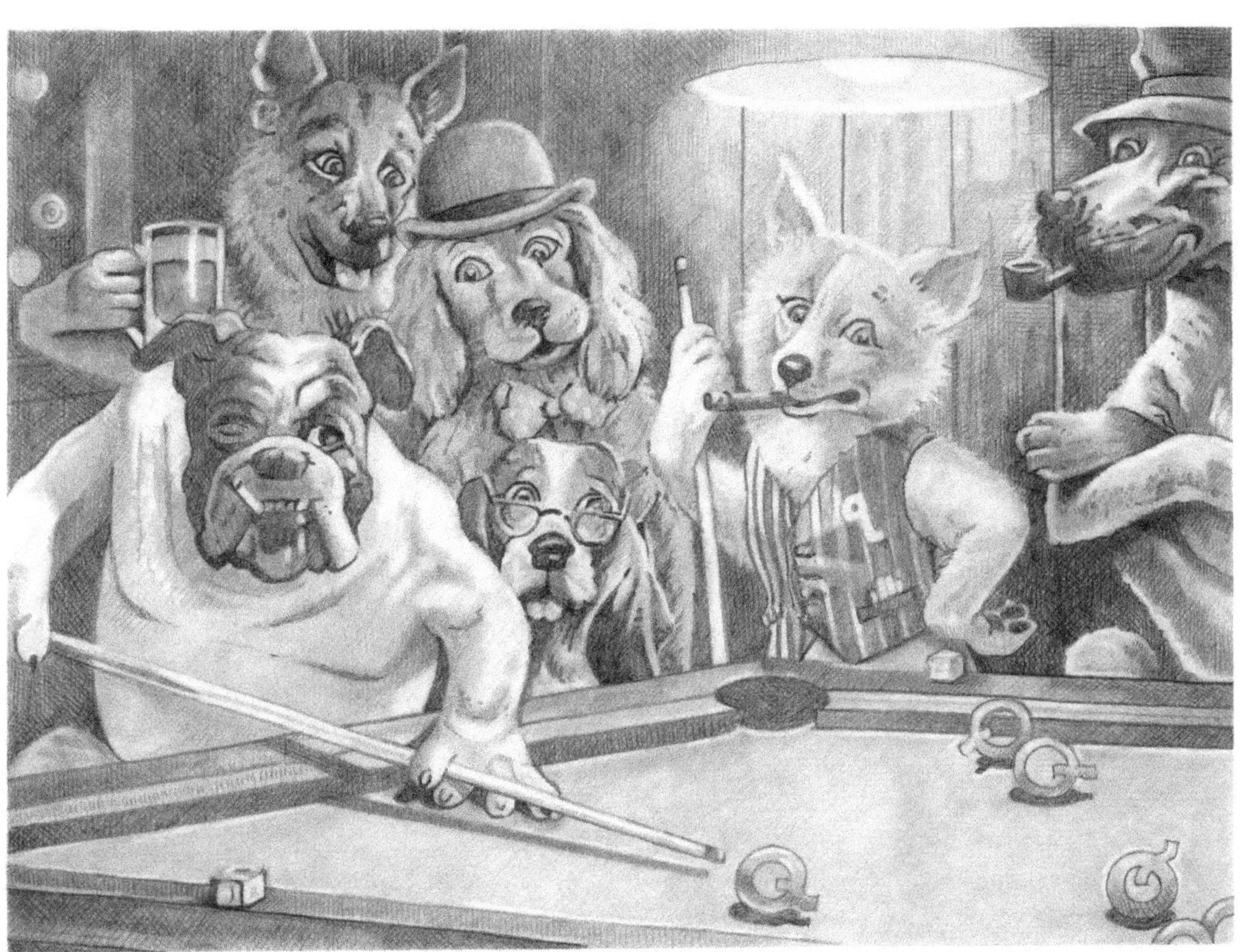

Art doesn't start with an R, and that's that.
If art started with R, we'd have Masters of Rat.

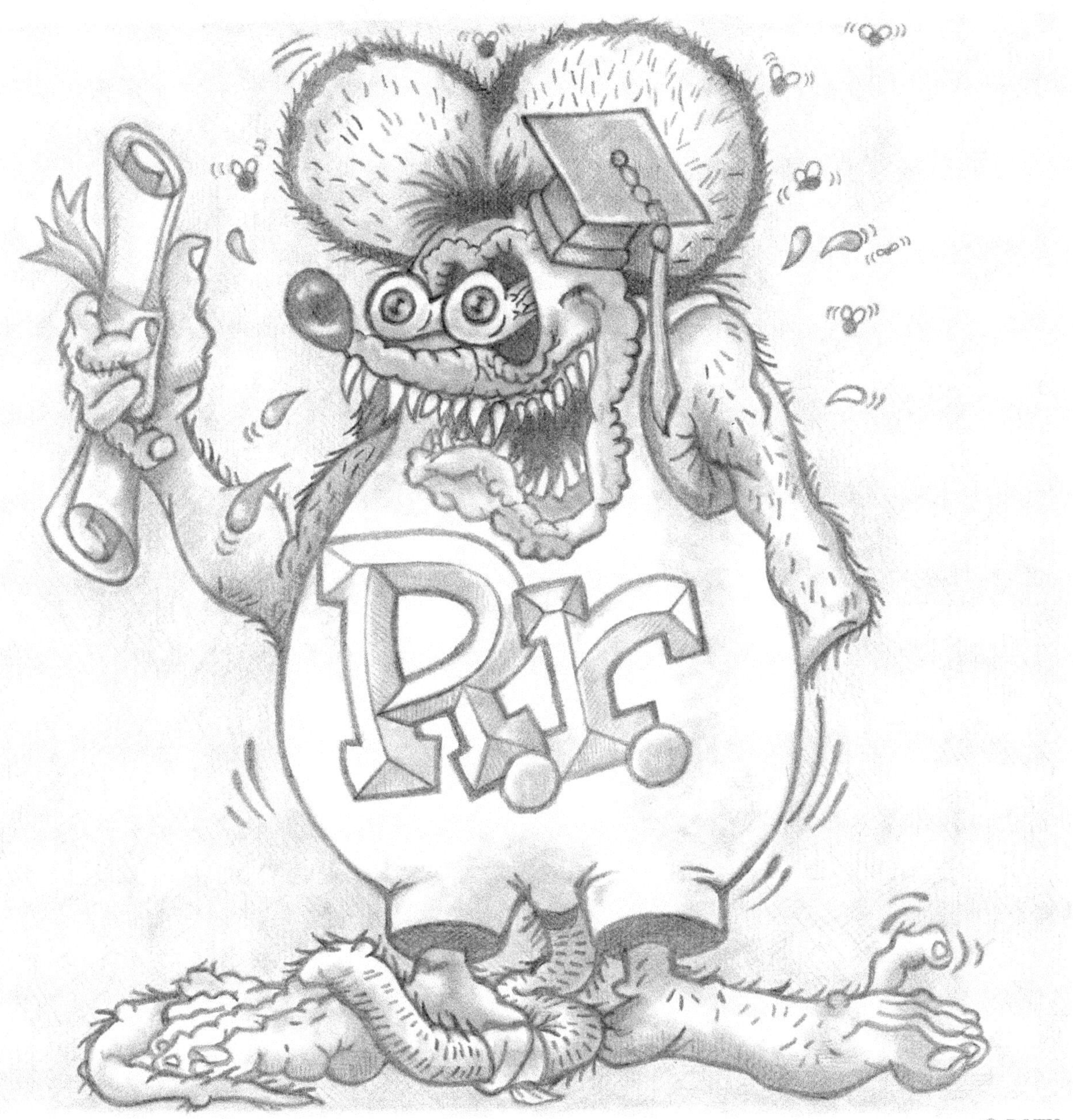
PhD
© ROTH

S is acidic; acidic as is.
Backwards or forwards, S is what S is.

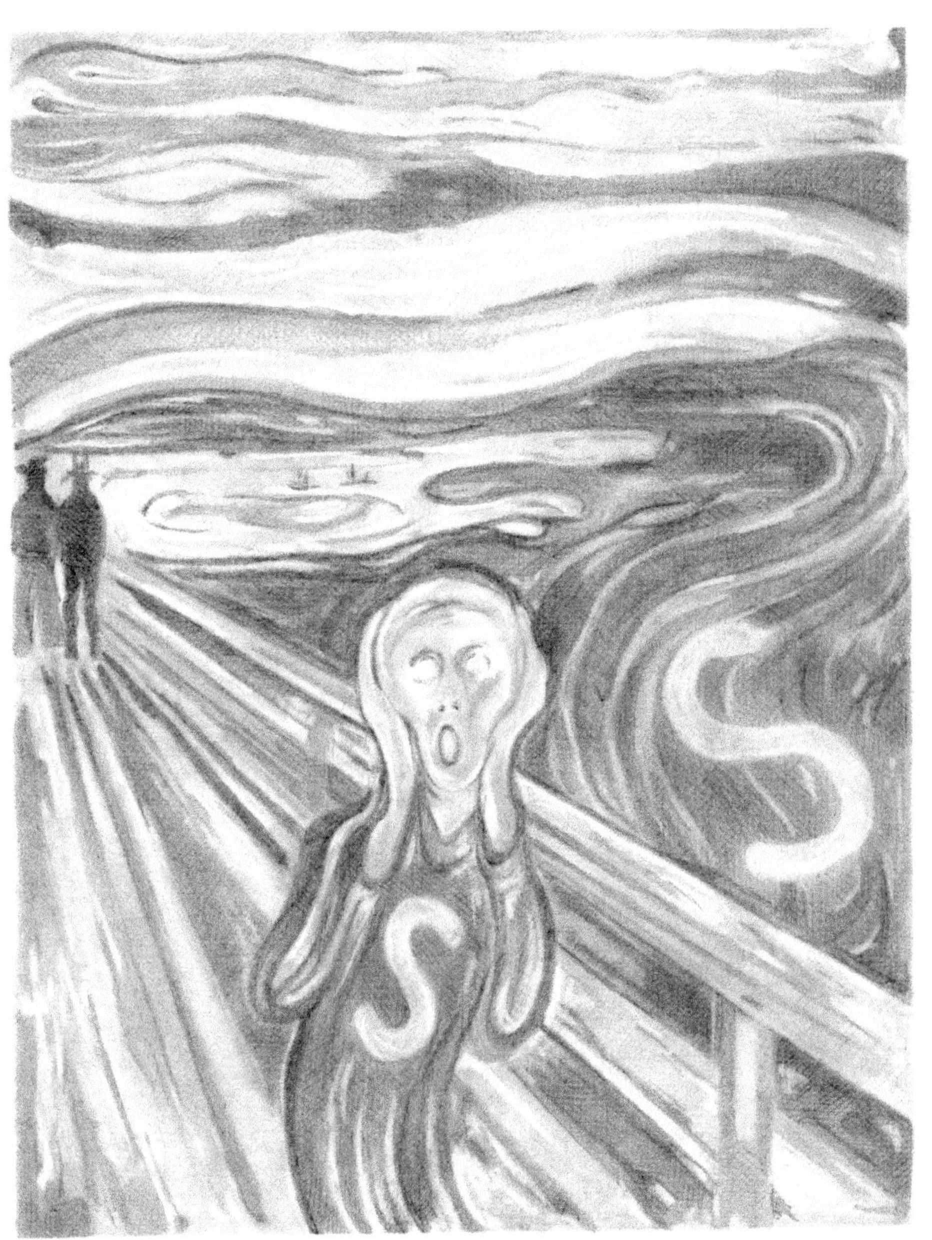

This is a thistle; these are all teasel.
This'll have two silent T's more than these'll.

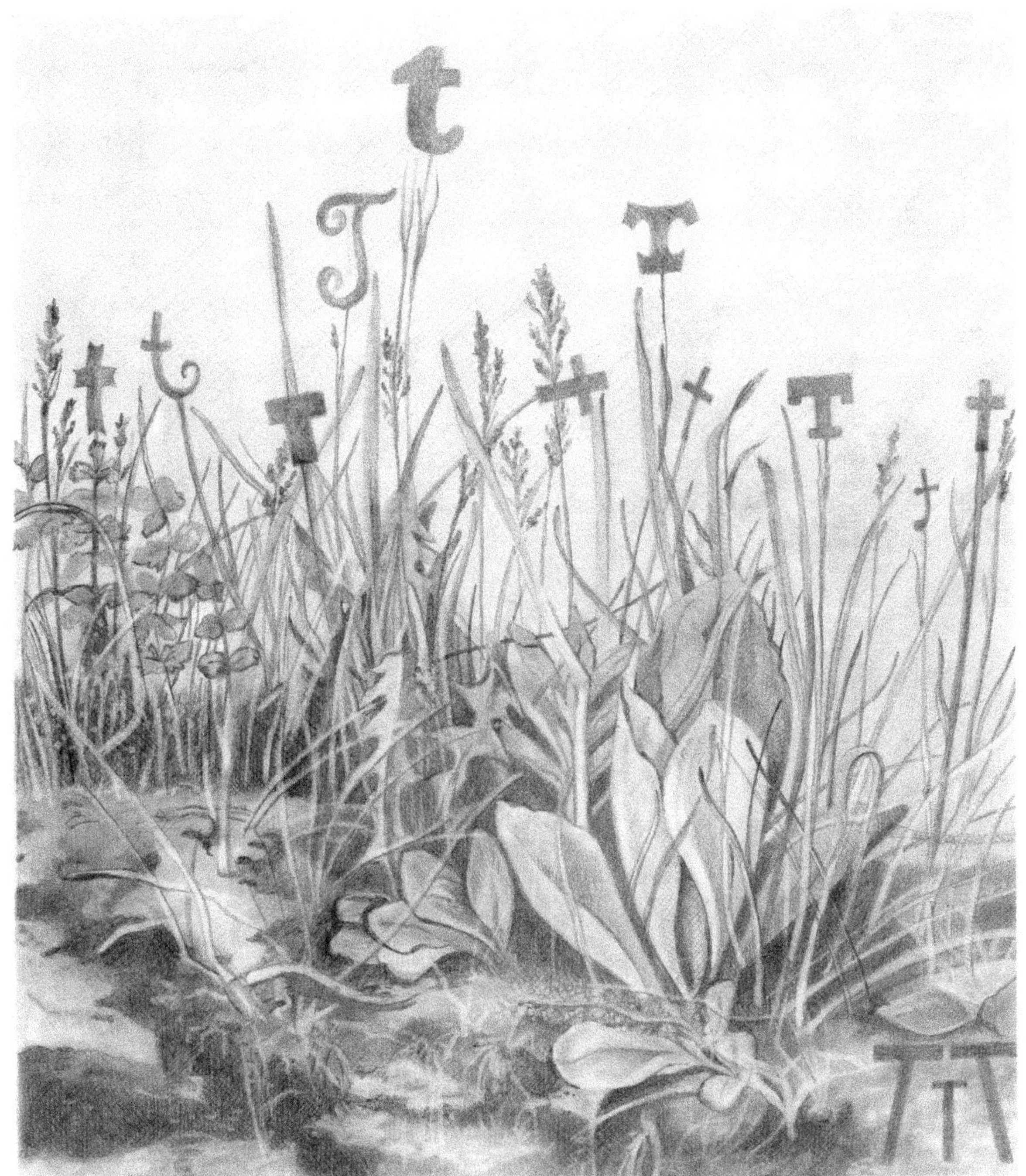

A ewe is a yew is a Eu. Is a U
Animal, vegetable...mineral, too?

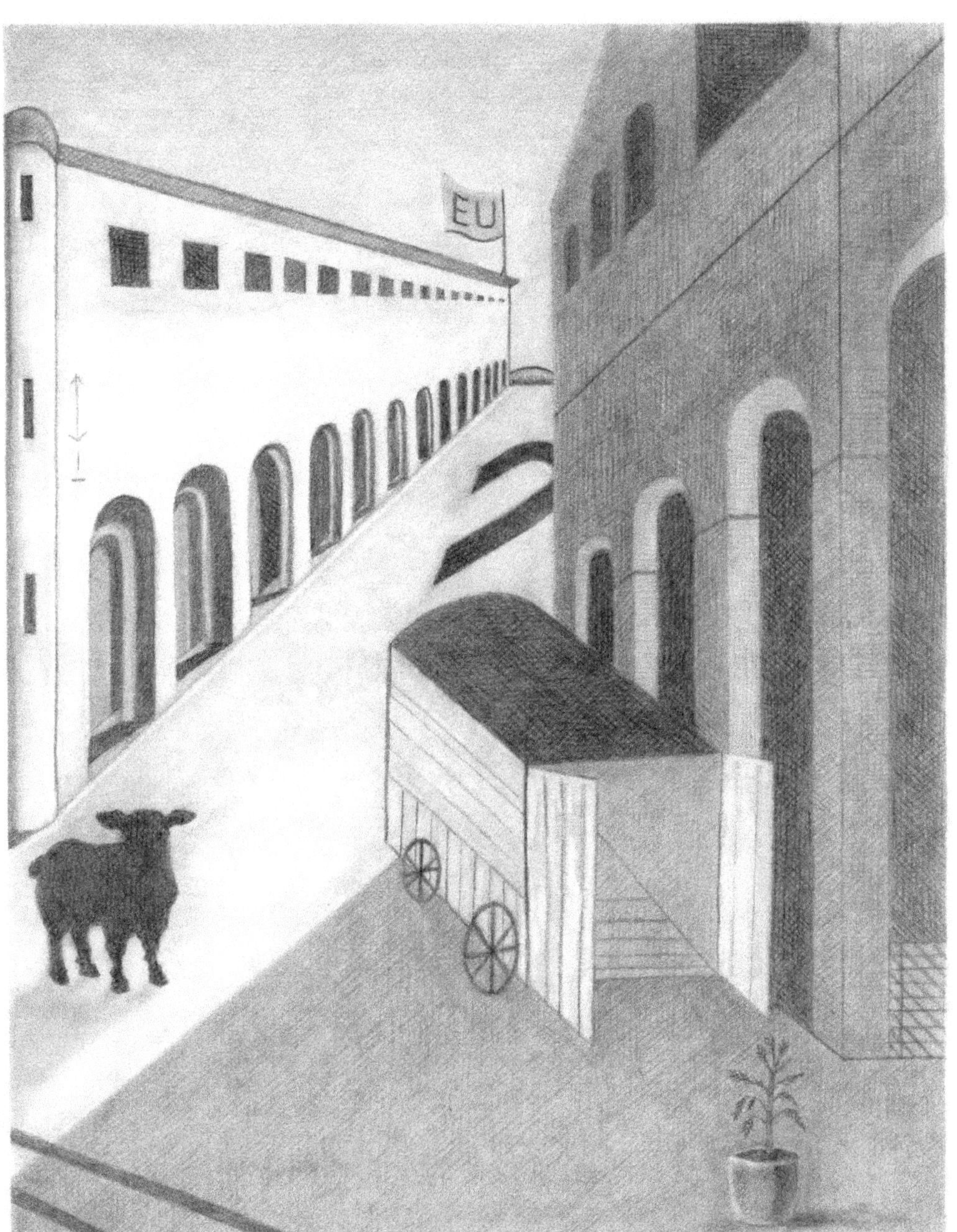

EU

V is for Wagner. Contrary to Greeley,
His word to young men was, "Goethe." I mean, really!

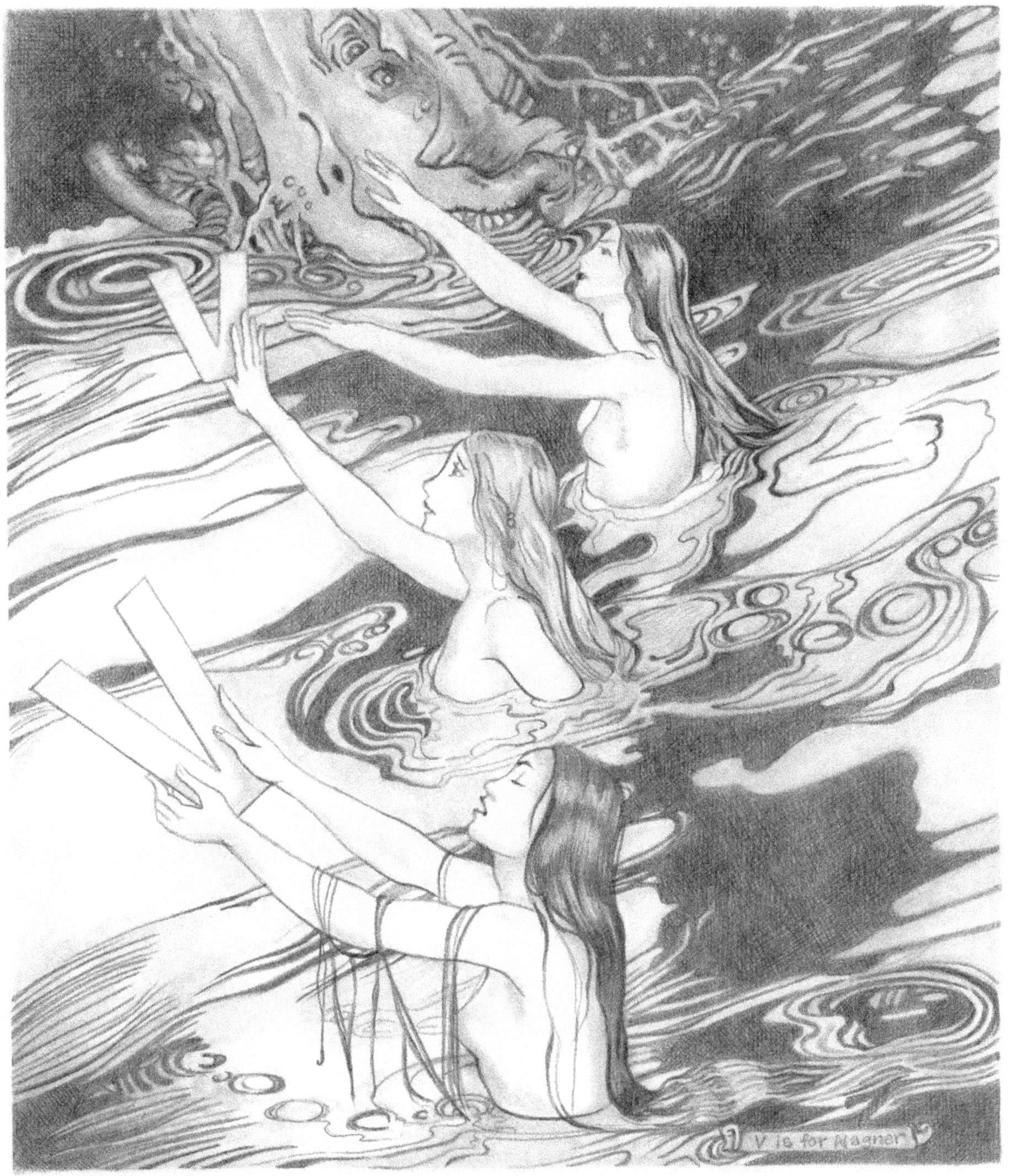
V is for Wagner

W? Vacuum! Does it trouble you
That we write double V, but then say double U?
If it were up to me, it would be double V.

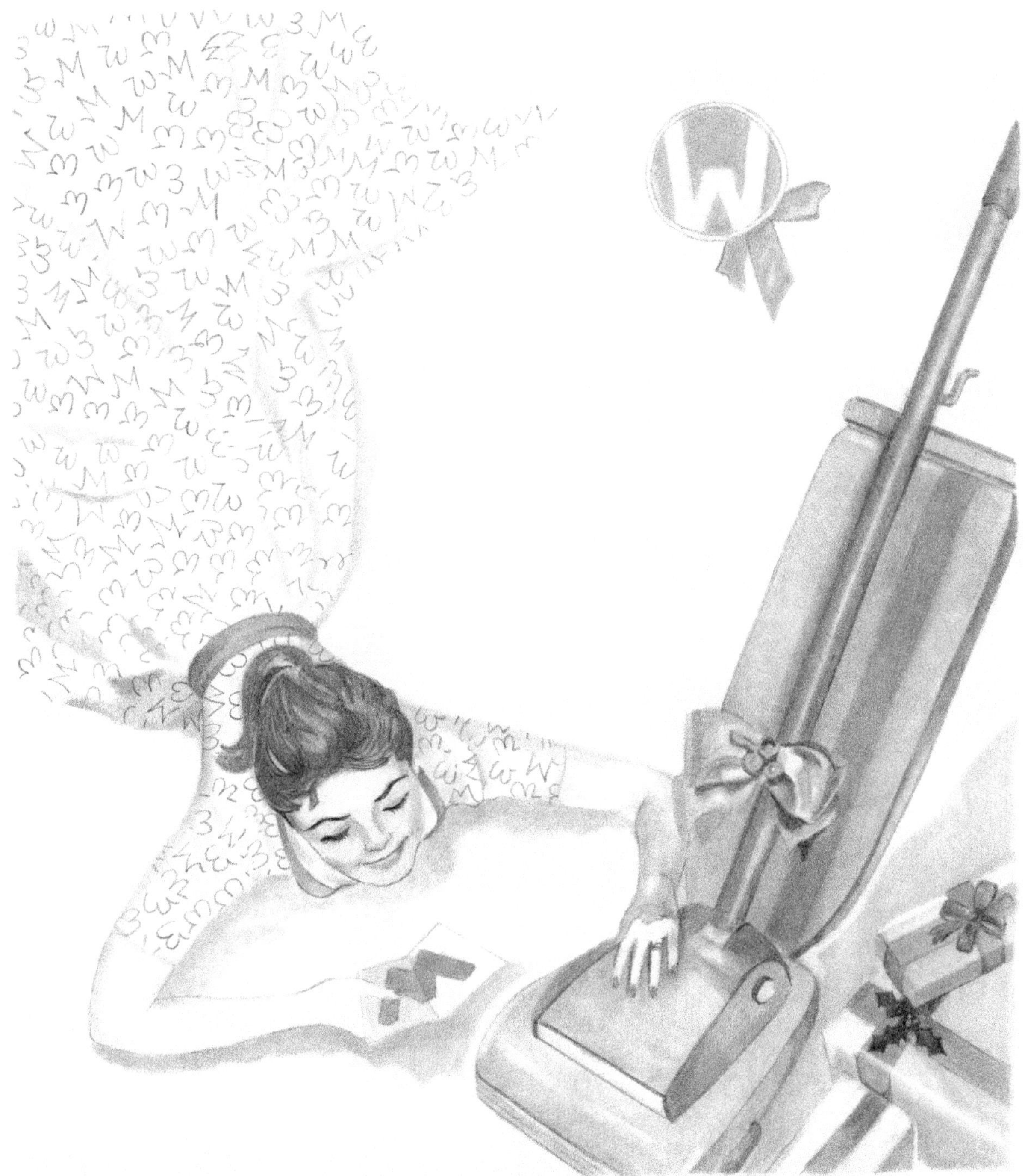

X is eccentric; it crosses the line
(It actually crosses two lines, by design).

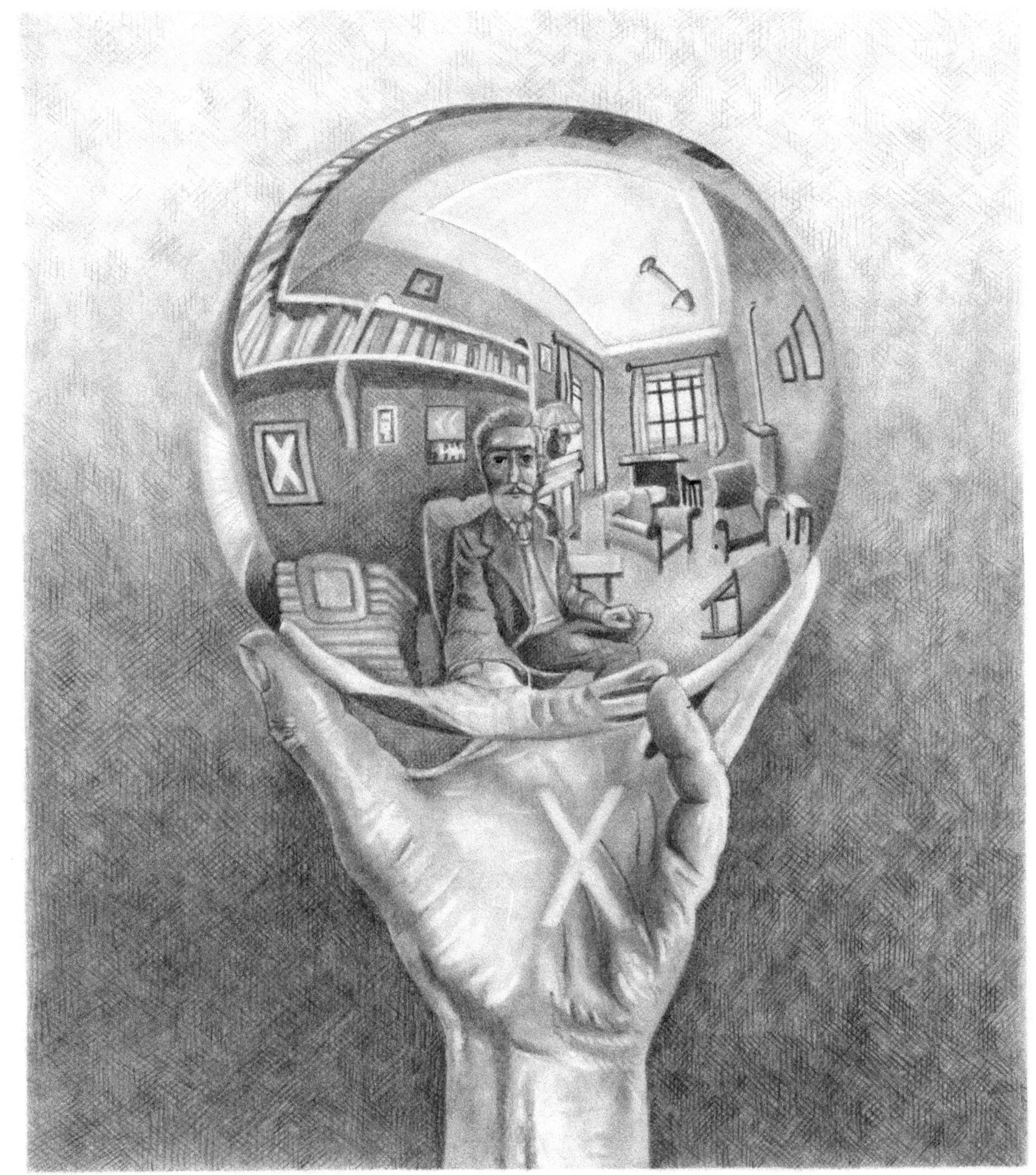

Neither early to bed, nor early to rise,
Will help a man spell the word "wise" using Y's.

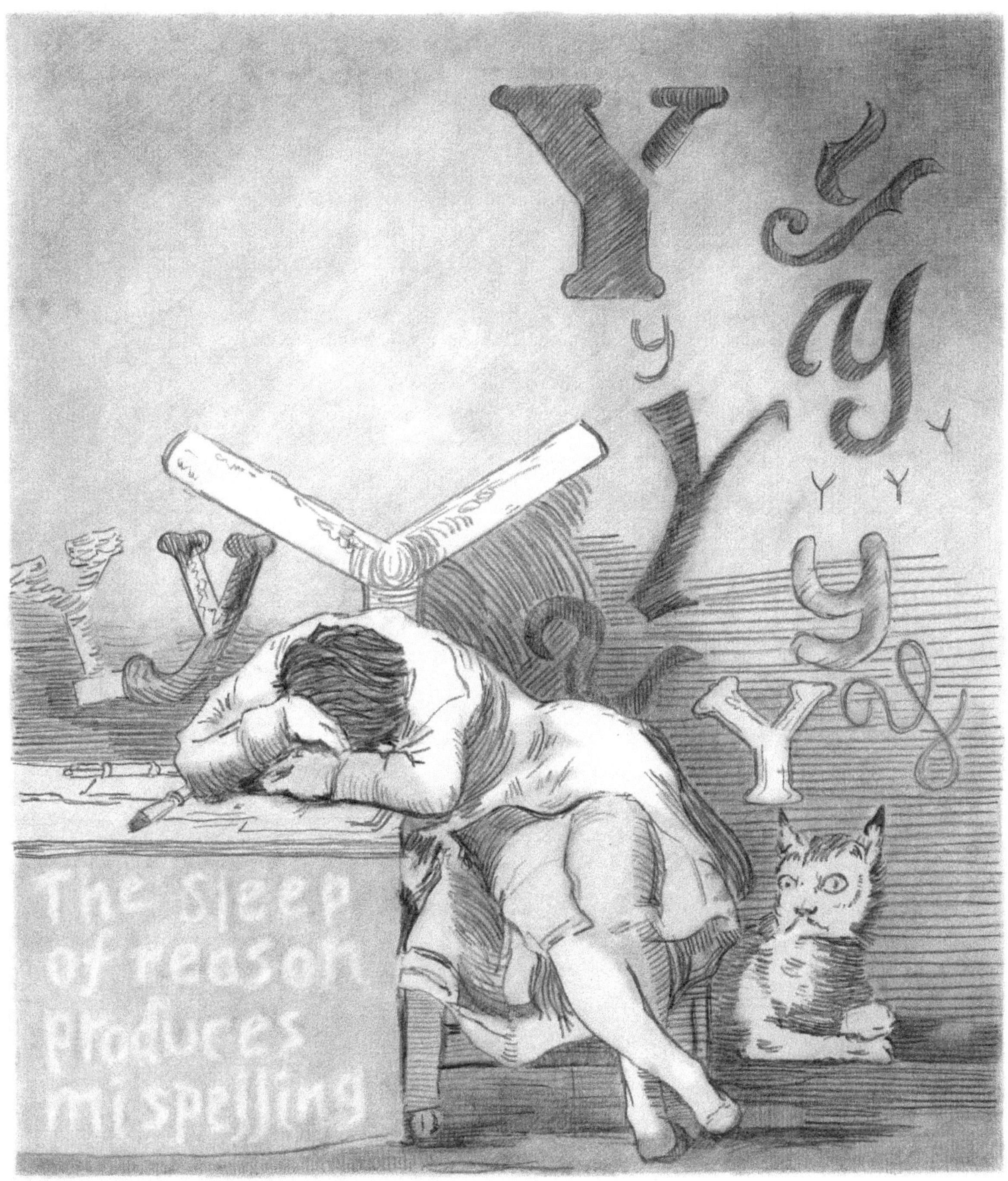

The sleep
of reason
produces
mispelling

Z: xenophobe. One who thinks it is wrong
For some things to be found where some others belong.
(The subject this alphabet raised all along.)

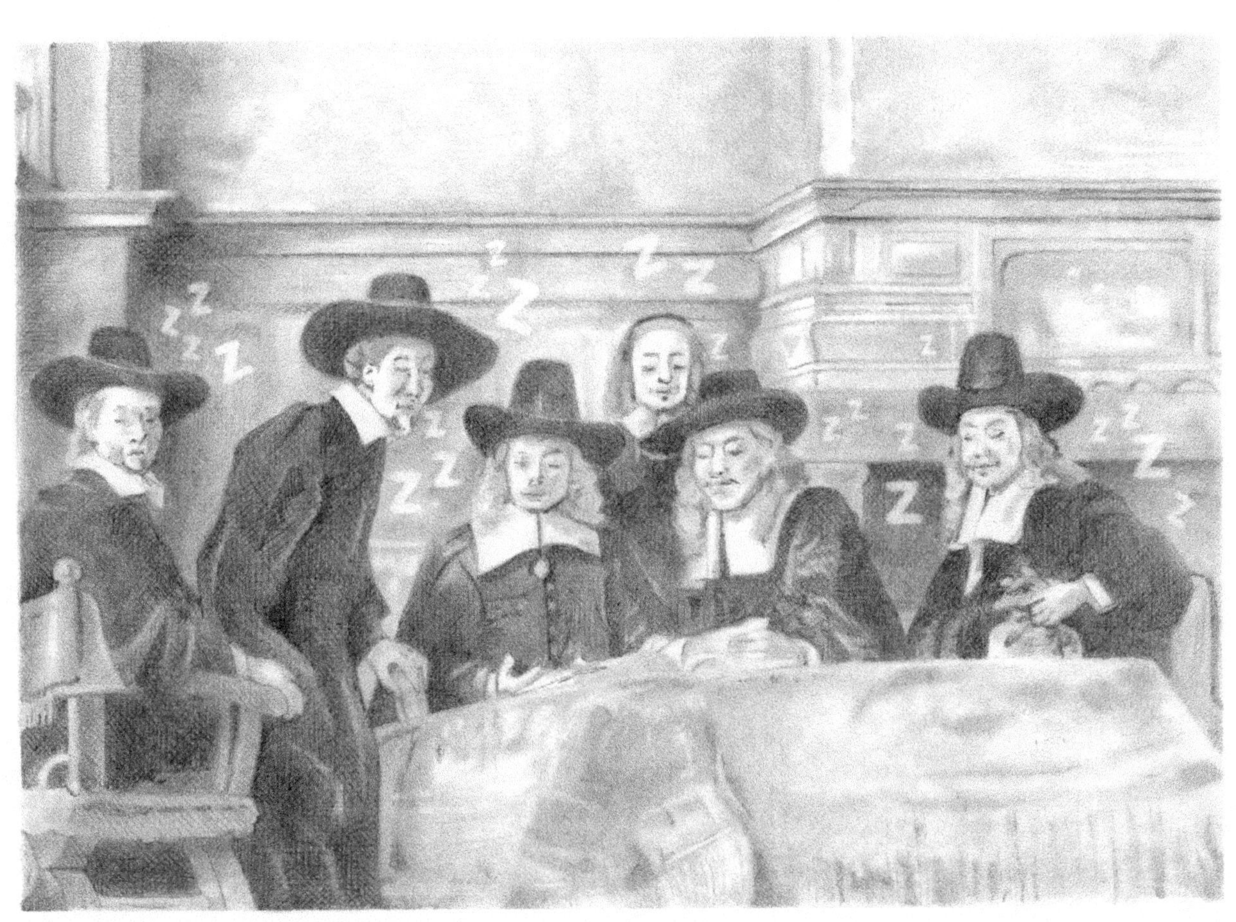

ART REFERENCES & INSPIRATIONS

A is inspired by Howard Terpning
Sound of Music, 1965
© The Rodgers & Hammerstein Organization

B is inspired by Michaelangelo
Bearded Slave, 1525 - 1530

C is inspired by John Bower
Battle of Fort McHenry, 1819

D is inspired by US Department of Justice
Al Capone Mugshot, 1931

E is inspired by Vincenzo Camuccini
The Death of Julius Caesar, 1806

F is inspired by Artist Unknown / Eric Litho and Printing Co.
Marvelo the Magician, 1911

G is inspired by an Unknown Artist
Mother Sewing With Her Two Children, 17th Century

H is inspired by Exekias
Achilles and Ajax Playing a Board Game, 540 - 530 B.C.

I is inspired by N. C. Wyeth
"Treasure Island" Book Illustration, 1911

J is inspired by Edgar Rubin
Rubin's Vase, 1915

K is inspired by Peter Paul Rubens
Cain Slaying Abel, 1608 - 1609

LMN is inspired by Paramount Pictures
"Top Secret!", 1984
Permission approval from Paramount Pictures
"The Skull" 1965 film which "Top Secret" parodied.

O is inspired by Vincent Van Gogh
Self Portrait with Bandaged Ear, 1889

P is inspired by Troma Entertainment, Inc.
"Toxic Avenger", 1984

Q is inspired Cassius Marcellus Coolidge/
Brown & Bigelow Advertising Company
Dogs Playing Pool, 1894

R is inspired by Big Daddy Roth
Rat Fink
The artwork is redrawn and based on the art of Big Daddy Roth.
© ROTH

S is inspired by Edvard Munch
The Scream, 1893

T is inspired by Albrecht Durer
Great Piece of Turf, 1503

U is inspired by Giorgio de Chirico / Private Collection
Mystery and Melancholy of a Street, 1914
This is a free and ironic interpretation of
Giorgio de Chirico's artistic work.

V is inspired by Arthur Rackham
"The Rhine Maidens" for Wagner's "Ring", 1910 - 1911

W is inspired by Artist Unknown / TTI Floor Care North American
Hoover Vintage Magazine Ad, November 30, 1953
© TTIFloorCare

X is inspired by M. C. Escher
Hand with Reflecting Sphere,1935
The artwork is redrawn and based on M.C. Escher's
"Hand with Reflecting Sphere".

Y is inspired by Francisco Goya
The Sleep of Reason Produces Monsters, 1797-1799

Z is inspired by Rembrandt
DeStaalmeesters or The Syndics of the Drapers' Guild, 1662

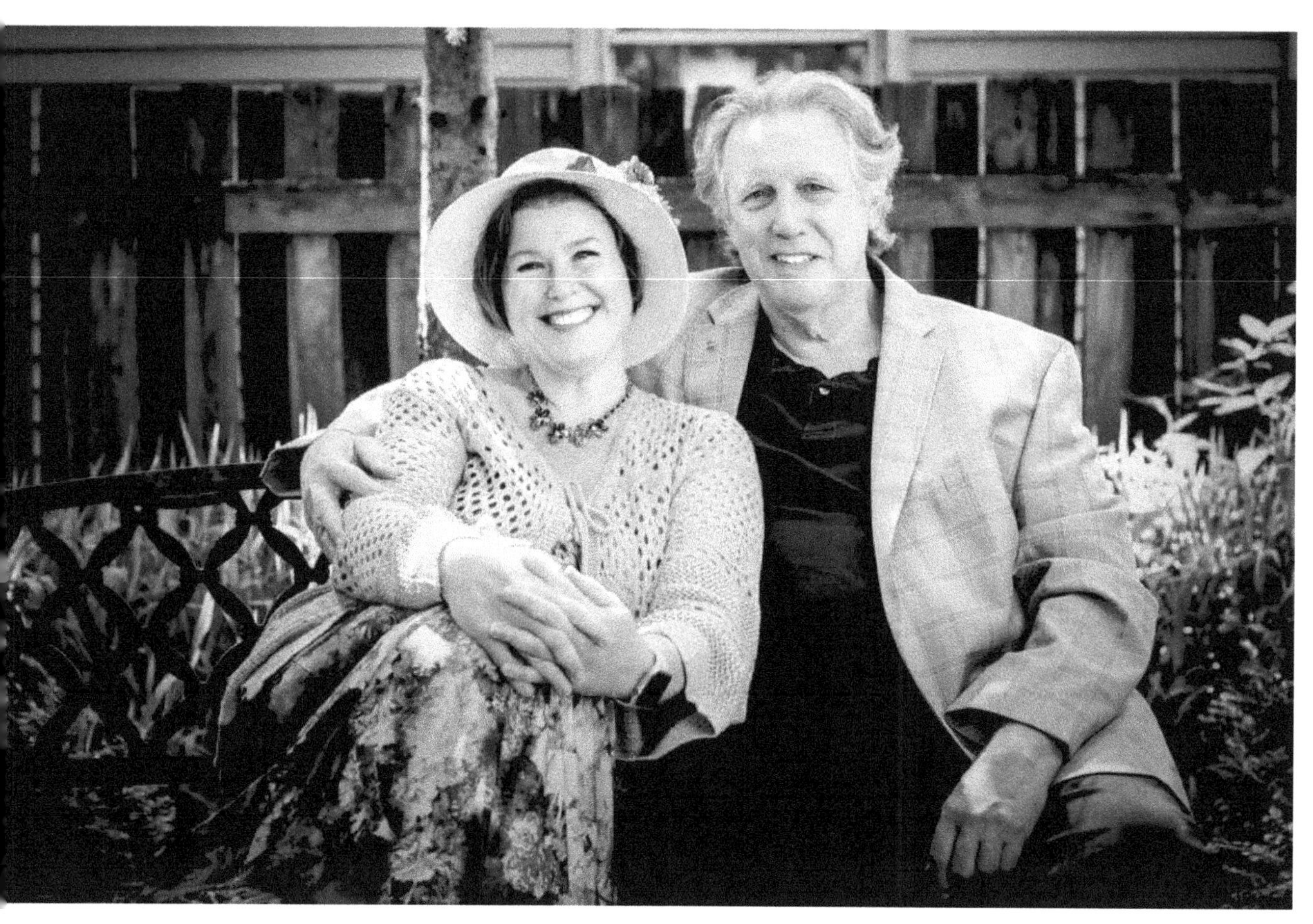

ABOUT THE BOOK

Jerald Eugene Noran could never understand why it took two different consonants to make the same sound in his first and second names. Or why his middle name didn't start with the letter U. Or why piano chords are written vertically and piano keyboards are oriented horizontally (but that's another story). This abecedarium is the result of decades of writing couplets, tercets, quatrains and sestains on tiny scraps of paper, regarding the inconsistencies of spelling and pronunciation in the English language. When did it become apparent that these scraps of paper could be compiled into an abecedarium? Not until it was done, because certain letters refused to be anything but ordinary. Typical for the English language: nothing is consistent, including its inconsistency.

ABOUT THE AUTHOR

Jerry Noran is a retired architect and building official whose professional experience centered on hospital renovation, accessibility projects, and building code consultation. None of this experience provided an outlet for his interest in constrained writing. Consequently, the borders of his desk calendars were filled with lists of palindromes, words with four consecutive vowels, homonyms that were also antonyms, Pilish poems and an assortment of peculiar limericks. His main winter project during retirement will be determining whether or not there is another book in these border scribblings. Jerry lives in Fort Thomas, Kentucky, with his wife, Cyndy, and their feline friend, Kitty Cat. Kitty Cat is not bothered by the fact that her first and second names require two different consonants in order to make the same sound. Jerry is.

ABOUT THE ILLUSTRATOR

Jennifer Noran is an artist who has many different outlets for self-expression including book illustrations, painting, costume design, sewing, sculpting, jewelry making and drawing. Her main inspirations are Maya Angelou and her world traveling Great Grandma Mabel. Both had a sense of adventure and made sure they lived their lives to the fullest. Jennifer currently works for the state of Kentucky as a graphic artist, but also is the president/ Queen Bee of the steampunk organization Queen City Steam (www.queencitysteam.com) and her graphics business JennyKat Productions (www.jennykat.com). Jennifer resides in Lexington, Kentucky, with her conservatory of plants at her little sanctuary and studio she calls home.